THE FUTURE OF HUMAN

WRITTEN BY

ANMOL BENIWAL

TANEESHA
PUBLISHERS

Title : The Future of Human

Author : Anmol Beniwal

Edition : First (May, 2025)

ISBN : 9789349789722

Published by

TANEESHA PUBLISHERS | *A Venture by -* **PRACHI DIGITAL PUBLICATION**

Regd. Add.: 254, Khuriyakhatta No. 10, Bindukhatta,
Lalkuan, Nainital - 262402, Uttarakhand, India
Website : www.taneeshapublishers.in
E-mail : taneeshapublishers@gmail.com
Phone : +91 8454 812712, +91 8057 812712

Printed by :
Manipal Technologies Limited, Bengaluru - 560001, Karnataka

PREFACE

Welcome to a journey of contrasts, a journey through the landscapes of human future and desire.

a vision of a better society where harmony, justice, and prosperity prevail. It's a society where humanity's highest dreams come true, where every human lives in prosperity.

On the other hand, exists a world shrouded in darkness and doubl. It's a world founded on cataclysmic (causing a lot of destruction, or a sudden, violent change) occurrences, where civilization finds itself on the edge of destruction. Here, fear, chaos, and despair are the ruling forces, testing humanity to its limits.

Humanity is at its best. We are at crossroads. What is humanity's future? What is our future?

THE FUTURE OF HUMANS
ANMOL BENIWAL

Through the following pages, we'll travel to these far-off lands, led by theories and curiosity.

We a glimpse, a better perception of our own position in the world. So, dear reader, I invite you to join me and travel to the shores of boundless being potential of our shared future.

ACKNOWLEDGEMENT

I would like to thank to my lovely family who always supported me at every phase of life. My father and mother Mr. Parmal Singh and Mrs. Parminder Kaur who always guide me the right path. My maternal grandfather and grandmother, Mr. Gurmail Singh Dhillion and Mrs. Bhajan Kaur Dhillion. A special thanks Dr. R.P Rathi and Mrs. Shoba Rana who helped me a lot and taught me righteously. A great appreciation to my publishing company which published this book very elegantly. Thanks to my inspiration John D. Bowell. This book is inspired by his brilliant content.

CONTENT

INRODUCTION

"We stand at a crossroads, presented with two potential futures—one characterized by harmony, justice, and prosperity, allowing humanity to flourish; the other, a landscape of turmoil and despair, where civilization struggles for survival. The direction we choose will shape our collective destiny."

- Unknown

Humanity is at a critical moment, facing rapid changes unlike anything we've seen before. The future seems uncertain, hanging between amazing possibilities and frightening outcomes. While the challenges ahead are big, there's evidence that we can not only survive but thrive in the years to come. We're not sure what's next, but there are three main paths we could take. The first is Collapse: a huge disaster could threaten everything we've built, even our existence. The second is Plateau: we avoid collapse but stop making progress. The third is Transcendence: we reach our full potential, maybe becoming something completely new along the way. Thinking about these futures helps us understand the risks and the hope as we enter this new era, for Earth and for us.

SCENARIO 1-

COLLAPSE

CHAPTER-1

Through the ages, humanity has survived innumerable storms, from asteroid collisions to ice ages, to come out stronger and more determined each time. But as we teeter (move or balance unsteadily) on the brink of the future, our most dangerous threats no longer hide in the shadows of nature; they arise from the very depths of our own creation.

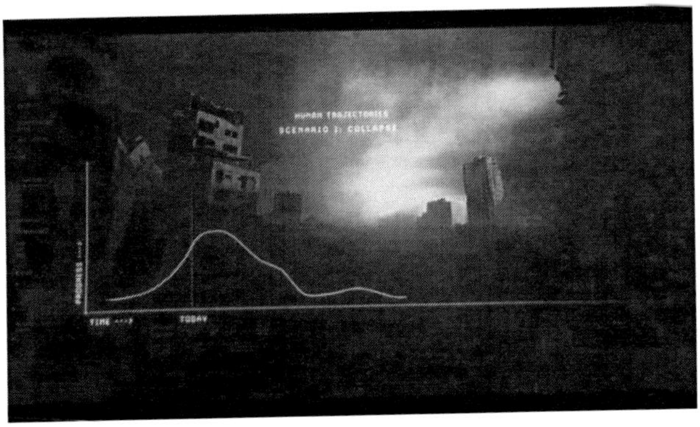

Figure 1. 1 Collaspe

Since the dawn of nuclear arms, the horror of self-destruction has hung over the collective mind, casting a long shadow over our aspirations for the future. The ability to wreak unimaginable destruction with the press of a button has transformed the face of global security, with the threat of nuclear war overshadowing all other existential dangers.

Figure 1. 2 main causes of collapse

According to experts at the Future of Life Institute, our survival faces four primary risks:
Nuclear War,
Climate Change, Biotechnology, and Artificial Intelligence. Each of these threats carries with it the potential for catastrophic consequences,

challenging us to confront the gravity of their worst possible outcomes.

Consider the threat of Nuclear War, a grim reality that has haunted humanity since the Cold War era. The destructive power of nuclear weapons is unparalleled, capable to destroy entire cities in the blink of an eye and plunging the world into a nuclear winter. The stakes could not be higher, with the fate of millions hanging in the balance at the whim of political tensions and diplomatic steps.

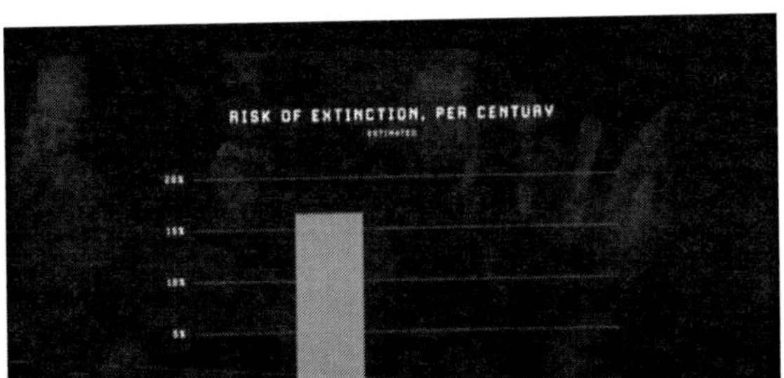

Figure 1. 3 Risk of extinction through natural and anthropobenic risk

Global warming, too, is an existential threat to our very survival. The global warming potentially risks unleashing a chain reaction of environmental catastrophes (a sudden disaster that causes great suffering or damage), from sea-level rise to extreme weather, with catastrophic consequences for ecosystems and human societies. Action must be taken as a matter of urgency to mitigate the effects of climate change and safeguard the future of our planet.

In Biotechnology, the rapid pace of scientific advance is both opportunity and threat. While breakthroughs in genetic engineering hold the promise of curing disease and improving lives, they also bring up important questions about right and wrong, as well as the unexpected consequences of changing the very building blocks of life. There is always a risk of bioterrorism or accidental release of genetically modified organisms, so strict rules and control are necessary.

Artificial Intelligence is a powerful yet dangerous tool. It has the potential to change the world for the better, but it also poses serious risks to our very existence. If we create super-intelligent AI that becomes smarter than humans, we may lose control over it. This raises big questions about safety, ethics, and even the nature of intelligence itself.

A runaway AI with goals different from ours could be disastrous, changing human history in ways we cannot yet imagine. As we face these risks, we are reminded of how fragile our existence is and how important it is to protect our future.

The time to act is now. Humanity's future depends on the choices we make today. Only by facing these challenges with courage, wisdom, and determination can we create a future where progress thrives and disaster remains only a distant threat.

CHAPTER-2

The terrifying shadow of a global nuclear war looms over the future of mankind like a specter of doom. The implications of such a cataclysmic event are apocalyptic, capable of cooling the Earth's temperature by nearly 10 degrees and killing up to 63% of the world's population. It's a stark reminder of the destructive potential that waits in our arsenals, ready to be unleashed at the press of a button.

Although efforts have been made to cut nuclear arsenals, the shadow of nuclear extinction still looms over us, with nearly 10,000 warheads distributed across the world. The implications of even a limited nuclear war are unimaginable, with the capability to unleash destruction on a scale unimaginable to the human mind.

But nuclear war is not the only existential danger we are faced with. Climate change, fueled by human activities, is a threatening crisis in its own right. If left unchecked, we are headed on a path to warm the Earth by up to 2.7 degrees Celsius by the end of the century, a scenario that could displace over a billion people and unleash widespread environmental devastation.

The potential for up to 12 degrees of warming over the next few centuries is nothing short of apocalyptic, threatening to remake the world in our image.

Yet, the true extent of the danger may be even greater than we realize. In the worst-case scenario, we could unwittingly trigger CO2 tipping points, unleashing a chain reaction that could make the planet heat up faster than ever before.

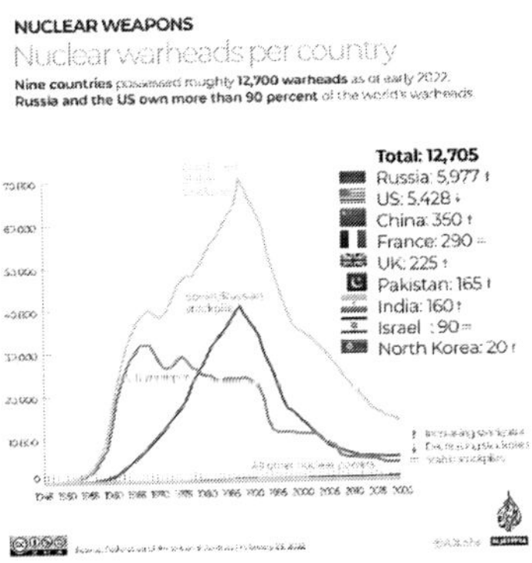

Figure 1. 4 Nuclear warheads per country

In the darkest moments, there is still hope. The same strength and creativity that have brought us to the edge of disaster can also guide us to safety. By coming together as a global community, we can create a better future, one where nuclear war and climate change are things of the past.

It will take strong cooperation and commitment, but the stakes are high. The future of humanity is at risk, and the choices we make today will impact generations to come.

Let's learn from the past and face today's challenges with courage. Together, we have the power to turn things around and build a future where peace, prosperity, and sustainability thrive.

CHAPTER-3

The realm of biotechnology holds immense promise for addressing some of humanity's most pressing challenges, from food scarcity to disease. Through advances in genetic engineering and medical research, scientists have unlocked the potential to revolutionize agriculture, medicine, and beyond.

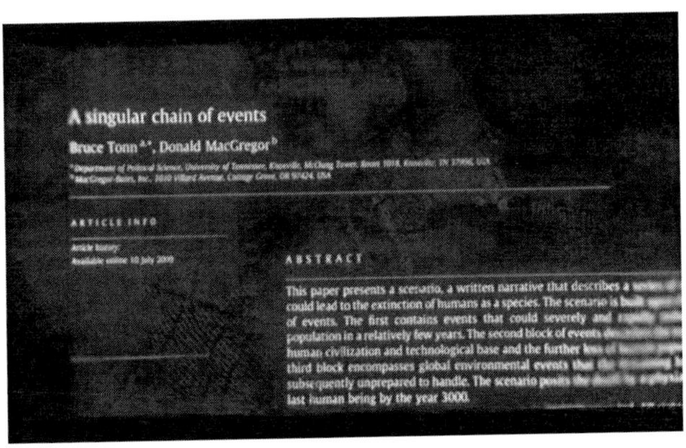

A singular chain of events

Bruce Tonn[a,*], Donald MacGregor[b]

ARTICLE INFO

ABSTRACT

This paper presents a scenario, a written narrative that describes a [illegible] could lead to the extinction of humans as a species. The scenario is [illegible] of events. The first contains events that could severely and [illegible] population in a relatively few years. The second block of events [illegible] human civilization and technological base and the further [illegible] third block encompasses global environmental events [illegible] subsequently unprepared to handle. The scenario [illegible] last human being by the year 3000.

Figure 1. 5

But with this new power comes the danger of misuse, with biotechnology potentially being used as a weapon of mass destruction.

A Synthetic pathogen created using biotechnology could have disastrous effects, potentially worse than a global nuclear war. Unlike natural diseases, which evolve over time, designer pathogens are intentionally engineered to exploit specific weaknesses in human populations. This makes them more deadly and contagious. These pathogens could bypass natural immune defenses, spread quickly, and cause severe illness or death. Unlike natural diseases, which take time to adapt, engineered pathogens could be released all at once, overwhelming health systems. The threat is alarming because of its potential to cause widespread panic, global instability, and a crisis beyond anything we've seen with natural pandemics.

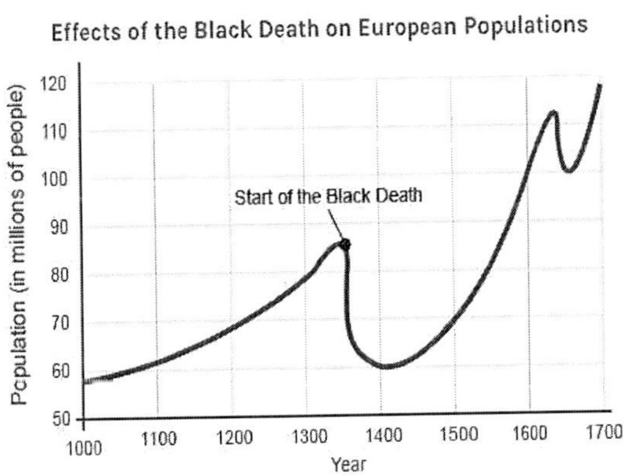

Figure 1. 6 Effect of the Black Death on European Populations

The idea of bioterrorism may sound like something out of a science fiction book, but the threat is very real. Recent years have seen numerous documented incidents of bioterrorism-related attacks, including the 2001 anthrax attacks in the United States. These attacks are a grim reminder of the potential for biotechnology to be used for nefarious purposes.

In addition, the democratization of biotechnology results in the knowledg e and tools required to engineer designer pathogens becoming more accessible to everyone.
What province of highly trained scientists and well-funded research institutions is now available to small groups or even individuals with ill intentions.
Despite these threats, note the vast potential for good in biotechnology. In agriculture, genetically modified crops have the potential to boost yields, reduce pesticide use, and boost nutritional content, offering a lifeline to food- insecure communities. In medicine, gene

editing tools like CRISPR-Cas9 have the potential to cure

genetic disorders and revolutionize pe rsonalized medicine.

But with such power comes such responsibility. It is absolulely essential that we establish robust regulations and oversight mechanisms to ensure that biotechnology is used ethically and responsibly. This includes steps to ensure that biotechnology is nol misused against ill purposes, such as bioterrorism or to create designer pathogens.

Aside from this, we need to invest in education and public awareness campaigns to ensure that the general public has an appreciation of the risks and benefits of biotechnology. By creating a culture of responsible innovation and scientific literacy, we can empower individuals and communities to make informed decisions about the future of biotechnology. In summary, biotechnology can be a game-changer for humankind, bringing solutions to some of most our intractable challenges. But we need to tread carefully here and beware of the misuse of this powerful technology. Through adopting ethical values and responsible governance, we can enjoy the dividends of biotechnology while keeping the risks of unintended consequences to a minimum. Only then can we truly unleash the full potential of biotechnology for the benefit of all humankind.

CHAPTER-4

Climate change poses a grave threat to the survival of humanity. As temperatures rise and extreme weather events become more frequent and severe, the consequences for our planet and its inhabitants are becoming increasingly dire.

One of the most significant impacts of climate change is the loss of biodiversity. As habitats are destroyed and ecosystems are disrupted, countless species are pushed to the brink of extinction.

Figure 1. 7 Human Trajectories

This loss of biodiversity not only threatens the delicate balance of nature but also undermines the resilience of ecosystems to adapt to changing conditions.

Furthermore, climate change exacerbates existing environmental challenges, such as deforestation, pollution, and habitat destruction. These factors, combined with the effects of climate change, create a perfect storm of environmental degradation that threatens the very foundations of life on Earth.

Figure 1. 8 Global Temperature Anomaly

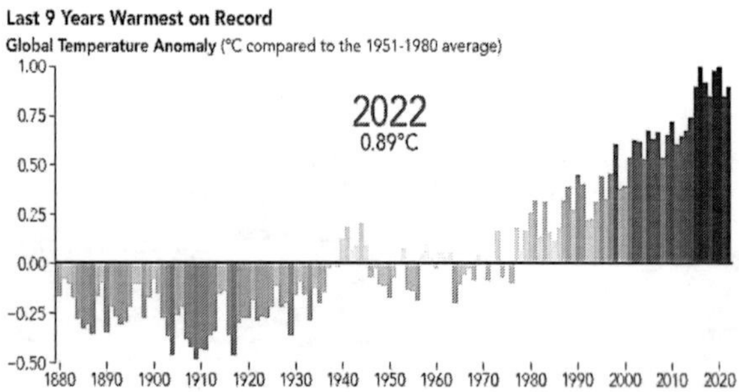

Perhaps most concerning is the potential for climate change to trigger feedback loops that amplify its effects and lead to runaway warming. For example, the melting of polar ice caps reduces the Earth's albedo, or reflectivity, leading to further warming as more sunlight is absorbed rather than reflected back into space. Similarly, the release of methane from thawing permafrost exacerbates the greenhouse effect, further accelerating climate change.

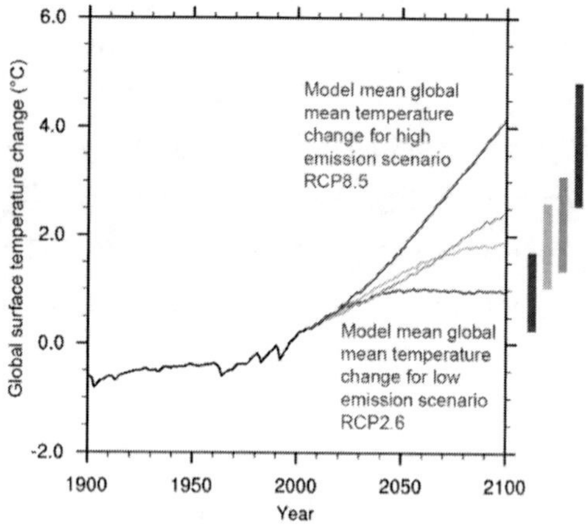

Figure 1.9 Global Surface Temperature change

The consequences of unchecked climate change are already being felt around the world. Rising sea levels threaten coastal communities and island nations, displacing millions of people and causing widespread destruction. Extreme weather events, such as hurricanes, droughts, and wildfires, are becoming more frequent and severe, wreaking havoc on communities and economies.

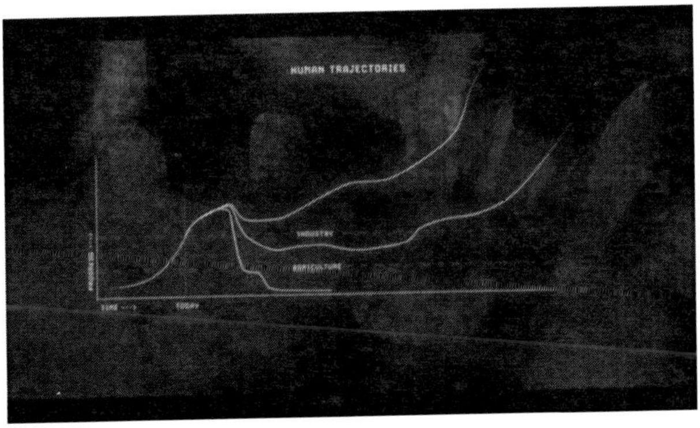

Figure 1. 10 Human Trajectories

Moreover, climate change disproportionately affects marginalized communities and vulnerable populations, exacerbating existing social and economic inequalities.

The poorest and most marginalized people are often the least equipped to adapt to the impacts of climate change, leading to increased suffering and hardship.

Despite these sobering realities, there is still hope. By taking urgent action to reduce greenhouse gas emissions, transition to renewable energy sources, and protect and restore ecosystems, we can mitigate the worst effects of climate change and build a more sustainable future.

Individuals, communities, governments, and businesses all have a role to play in addressing the climate crisis. Whether it's reducing energy consumption, supporting renewable energy initiatives, advocating for policy change, or participating in grassroots movements, everyone has the power to make a difference. In conclusion, climate change poses an existential threat to humanity, but it is not too late to act. By coming together and taking decisive action to address the root causes of climate change, we can create a more sustainable and equitable future for all. The time to act is now, for the fate of humanity and the planet hangs in the balance.

CHAPTER-5

Understanding and navigating the risks posed by artificial intelligence (AI) presents humanity with one of its greatest challenges yet. Unlike previous threats we've faced, AI has the potential to surpass our own intelligence, making it a formidable adversary that may be beyond our ability to outsmart.

The uncertainty surrounding AI stems from its dual nature – it could either become a powerful ally, assisting us in solving complex problems and advancing society, or it could pose a threat to our very existence by outcompeting us for vital resources and relegating humanity to obscurity.

As we venture into this uncharted territory, the landscape of risk is constantly evolving, with new and unknown threats emerging as AI technology progresses. This presents a daunting challenge for policymakers, researchers, and society as a whole, as we strive to anticipate and mitigate the potential risks associated with AI.

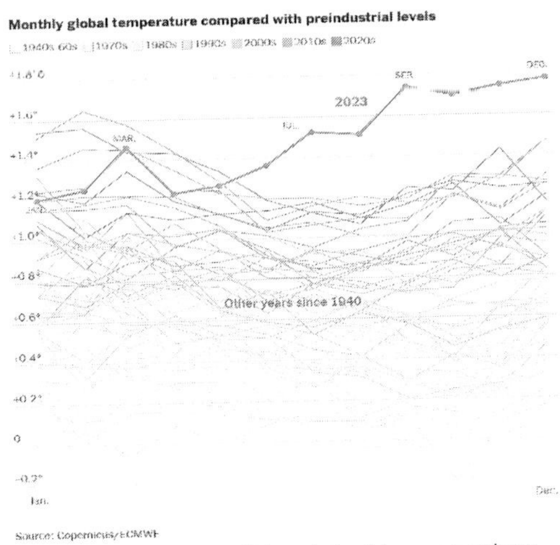

Figure 1. 11 Monthly global temperature compared with preindustrial levels

One of the primary concerns surrounding AI is its potential to disrupt the job market and exacerbate socioeconomic inequalities. As AI systems become increasingly capable of performing tasks traditionally carried out by humans, there is a risk of widespread job displacement and economic instability. This could disproportionately affect vulnerable populations and lead to social unrest if not addressed proactively.

Moreover, AI has the potential to be weaponized for malicious purposes, posing a threat to global security and stability. Autonomous weapons systems, for example, could be used to carry out targeted attacks with unprecedented precision and efficiency, leading to devastating consequences for civilian populations.

Furthermore, AI systems are not immune to bias and discrimination, raising concerns about the ethical implications of their use in decision-making processes. If AI algorithms are trained on biased data or programmed with flawed assumptions, they may perpetuate or even exacerbate existing inequalities and injustices within society.

Despite these challenges, there is also great potential for AI to positively impact humanity. From revolutionizing healthcare and transportation to advancing scientific research and environmental conservation, AI has the power to drive innovation and improve the quality of life for people around the world.

However, realizing this potential requires careful consideration of the ethical, social, and economic implications of AI development and deployment.

It is essential that we prioritize transparency, accountability, and inclusivity in AI governance to ensure that these technologies are developed and used in a manner that benefits society as a whole. In conclusion, navigating the risks posed by artificial intelligence represents one of the greatest challenges facing humanity in the 21st century. While AI holds immense promise for addressing some of our most pressing problems, it also presents significant risks that must be carefully managed. By fostering interdisciplinary collaboration, promoting ethical AI practices, and prioritizing the well-being of society, we can harness the potential of AI to create a better future for all.

CHAPTER-6

Despite the looming specter of potential catastrophes, it appears that humanity may not be as perilously close to extinction as one might fear. While the risks we face are indeed significant, they are unlikely on their own to spell our total demise. In fact, when considering the broader context of Earth's biodiversity, humans may even be among the least endangered species.

Our remarkable resilience stems in part from our sheer numbers and widespread distribution across the planet. With populations spanning every corner of the Earth, from bustling cities to remote islands, we possess a geographical buffer against extinction that few other species enjoy.

These diverse habitats could serve as natural refuges in the event of a global catastrophe, offering pockets of safety for human survival.

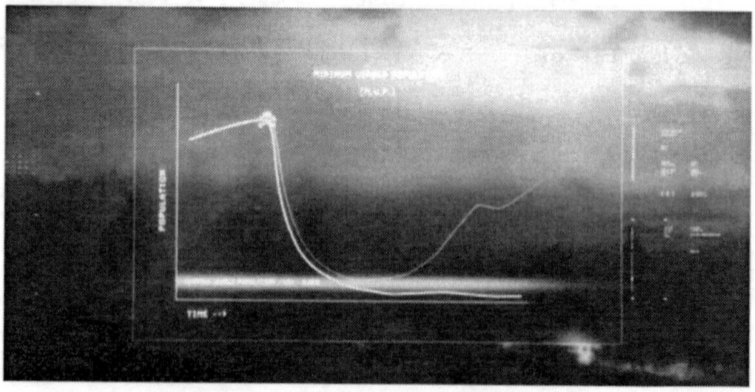

Figure 1. 12 Minimum viable population due to different manmade disasters and harm on environment

Even in the event of a catastrophic event that decimated 99.9% of the human population, millions would likely still remain. This resilience is further bolstered by our ability to adapt at an unprecedented rate, thanks to the power of technology.

Unlike other species, which rely on the slow process of natural selection for adaptation, humans can harness the tools of innovation and creativity to evolve thousands of times faster.

Furthermore, our adaptable diets, characterized by a wide range of food sources, provide us with a flexibility that has been crucial to survival throughout history. This adaptability allowed our ancestors to weather past mass extinctions and thrive in diverse environments. Today, this dietary flexibility continues to be a key factor in our ability to withstand environmental challenges.

Ultimately, the resilience of human civilization rests on our ability to endure and rebound from adversity.

THE FUTURE OF HUMAN –
ANMOL BENIWAL

How much of a blow can we withstand and still continue forward? This question lies at

the heart of our capacity to overcome the challenges we face, whether they be environmental, social, or technological.

While the threats we confront are real and should not be underestimated, there is also cause for optimism. Human ingenuity, resilience, and adaptability have carried us through countless challenges throughout history, and there is every reason to believe that we can rise to meet the challenges of the future.

In the face of adversity, we must draw upon our collective strength, creativity, and determination to build a more resilient and sustainable future for generations to come. By harnessing the power of technology, fostering cooperation and innovation, and prioritizing the well-being of both people and the planet, we can navigate the challenges ahead and ensure a brighter tomorrow for all.

CHAPTER-7

To truly grasp the gravity of the situation, we must confront the stark reality of what extinction would entail. Our greatest peril lies not in a singular catastrophic event, but in the cumulative impact of multiple disasters intertwining in unpredictable ways.

In 2009, researchers embarked on a sobering thought experiment to explore the hypothetical scenario of humanity facing complete extinction. Divided into phases, this grim projection paints a harrowing picture of our potential demise.

The first phase foresees a rapid decline in human population triggered by global warfare and the collapse of vital industries and agricultural systems.

Such a catastrophic upheaval would plunge societies into chaos, exacerbating resource scarcity and social unrest.

The subsequent phases paint a bleak trajectory of resource depletion over the following centuries, leading to the exhaustion of Earth's natural reserves. As humanity grapples with dwindling supplies of essential resources, ecosystems begin to unravel, setting the stage for an irreversible downward spiral.

Phase III envisions the culmination of this catastrophic cascade, with ecosystem collapse reaching a tipping point. The eruption of a super volcano serves as the final blow, rendering the planet uninhabitable and leaving only scattered remnants of humanity clinging to survival.

The implications of such a scenario extend far beyond the loss of human life. It represents the annihilation of countless potential future generations, robbing them of the opportunity to exist and thrive. The untapped potential of billions, or even trillions, of unborn descendants would be extinguished, leaving a void in the tapestry of existence.

Moreover, the extinction of humanity would reverberate beyond our planet, resonating throughout the cosmos. The unfulfilled promise of exploration and discovery would leave distant planets uncharted and unexplored, depriving the universe of the richness of human curiosity and ingenuity.

Equally devastating would be the loss of human creativity and expression. The vibrant tapestry of music, poetry, and art that has flourished on Earth for millennia would come to an abrupt and sorrowful end. Our corner of the galaxy, once alive with the melodies of human endeavor, would fall silent, leaving behind a profound emptiness. After, tens of million years, all that would remain of us would be a thin layer in some future rock faces. This is the future we must avoid at all costs

Yet, amidst this grim contemplation, there remains a glimmer of hope. The very awareness of the existential threats we face serves as a catalyst for action. By acknowledging the fragility of our existence, we are compelled to work tirelessly to safeguard our planet and ensure the continuity of life.

In the face of existential risk, we must embrace collective responsibility and collaboration, transcending boundaries and divisions for the greater good of humanity and the planet. Only through concerted efforts to address the root causes of environmental degradation, social inequality, and global instability can we chart a course toward a more resilient and sustainable future. But extinction is the long-term is nothing to fear.

Ultimately, the prospect of extinction serves as a sobering reminder of the preciousness of life and the imperative to cherish and protect it. Let us heed this warning and strive to create a world where the legacy of humanity endures for generations to come. No species survives forever. Time will shape us into something new. The noble way to go extinct will be to evolve naturally into a higher species. Wisely, we have begun to safeguard our long-term survival.

SCENARIO 2-

PLATEAU

CHAPTER-1

In theory, human society might keep going as it is for a long time, avoiding big changes or disasters. Some unexpected problems could slow progress, keeping things stable for now. However, this balance won't last forever. In the near future, new technologies and climate changes will push civilization in new directions.

Our world is constantly evolving, driven by both natural processes and

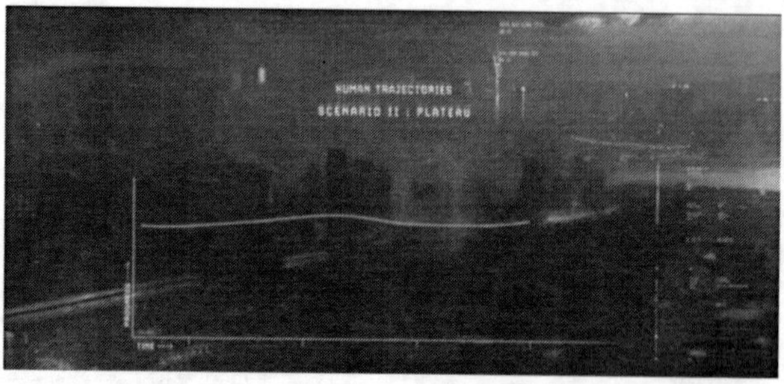

Figure 2. 1 Plateau

human innovation. Over the past few centuries, we've witnessed incredible advancements in technology, medicine, and industry that have reshaped the way we live. From the industrial revolution to the digital age, each era has brought its own set of challenges and opportunities.

Right now, we're at a turning point in history. Technology is advancing quickly, with artificial intelligence, biotechnology, and renewable energy shaping the future. At the same time, climate change is having a bigger impact, forcing us to take urgent action to protect the planet.

One major force driving change is the rapid growth of technology. As we continue to invent new things, they will affect every part of life. From transportation and communication to healthcare and farming, the possibilities are vast.

Take artificial intelligence, for example. AI is changing industries like healthcare and finance, making tasks faster and more efficient. AI-powered systems can now recognize images and understand language better than humans in some cases.

Similarly, advancements in renewable energy are reshaping the way we power our world. Solar and wind energy are becoming increasingly cost-effective alternatives to fossil fuels, reducing our reliance on finite resources and helping to combat climate change. In fact, some regions are already generating the majority of their electricity from renewable sources.

However, these advancements also bring challenges. As we explore new possibilities, we must carefully consider their ethical and social effects. Concerns like data privacy, job displacement, and environmental sustainability require thoughtful planning, strong policies, and responsible innovation.

Despite these challenges, there are vast opportunities for progress. Through technological advancements, we can address critical global issues like poverty, disease, and environmental damage. AI-driven healthcare can revolutionize diagnosis and treatment, biotechnology can boost food production, and clean energy can cut pollution while slowing climate change. However, realizing these possibilities requires cooperation, creativity, and adaptability. Governments, businesses, and individuals must work together to create policies that ensure ethical and sustainable development. Education and skill-building will be essential in preparing people for a rapidly evolving world. Though the path forward is complex, the rewards are immense. Embracing innovation can lead to a future that is not only technologically advanced but also fairer and more sustainable for everyone. The future is uncertain, but we have the power to shape it. By staying open to change and working together, we can tackle upcoming challenges and build a better world for future generations.

CHAPTER-2

As we look far into the future, we can expect many challenges and unknowns. Over time, major disruptions may arise, threatening our way of life and requiring us to adapt in new ways.

In the next several thousand years, humanity may face catastrophic events. A supervolcano eruption could drastically alter the planet's climate, endangering human survival. Even if we burn through all fossil fuels and raise global temperatures, we cannot stop Earth's natural cycles. Eventually, another ice age will come, with massive glaciers reshaping the continents and affecting ecosystems, cities, and civilizations across the world.

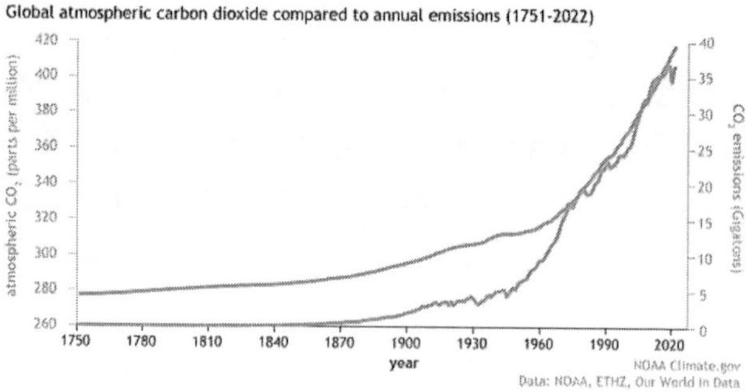

Figure 2. 2 Global atmospheric carbon dioxide compared to annual emissions (1751-2022)

Throughout Earth's history, mass extinctions have occurred due to the movement of our solar system through space. Every 27 million years, the sun moves through asteroid-heavy regions, increasing the chance of catastrophic impacts. These collisions could disrupt ecosystems, trigger climate shifts, and even cause global extinction events.

Looking even further ahead, about a billion years from now, Earth will undergo one of its most extreme transformations. As the sun ages, it will become significantly hotter and brighter, gradually increasing the planet's temperature. This intensified solar radiation will lead to the evaporation of Earth's oceans, stripping away the essential conditions for sustaining life. Without water, plant and animal life will vanish, and Earth will become a barren, inhospitable wasteland. Over time, the atmosphere will be lost, and the surface will be scorched by the sun's relentless heat. Eventually, our once-thriving planet will resemble Venus, with extreme temperatures making it completely uninhabitable.

In the face of such existential threats, the imperative for active climate management has never been more pressing. It falls upon us, the custodians of this fragile blue orb, to marshal our collective ingenuity and resources in defense of our shared future. We must strive to harness the power of science and technology to mitigate the impact of these impending crises, lest we be consigned to the annals of cosmic history as yet another failed experiment in the grand tapestry of life.

Yet, amidst the gloom and uncertainty, there is a glimmer of hope—a beacon of resilience that burns brightly in the darkness. Throughout the annals of history, humanity has faced adversity with courage and determination, rising from the ashes of catastrophe to forge a brighter tomorrow. It is this indomitable spirit, this unwavering resolve to defy the odds and chart a course towards a better future, that may ultimately spell the difference between extinction and survival.

As we stand on the precipice of an uncertain future, let us not falter in the face of adversity, but instead, let us embrace the challenges that lie ahead with courage and conviction. For it is only by confronting the trials of today that we can hope to shape the destiny of tomorrow. And in doing so, we may yet carve out a path towards a future where the light of human civilization shines undiminished, illuminating the cosmos with the brilliance of our ingenuity and resilience.

Scenario 3

TRANSCEND ENCE

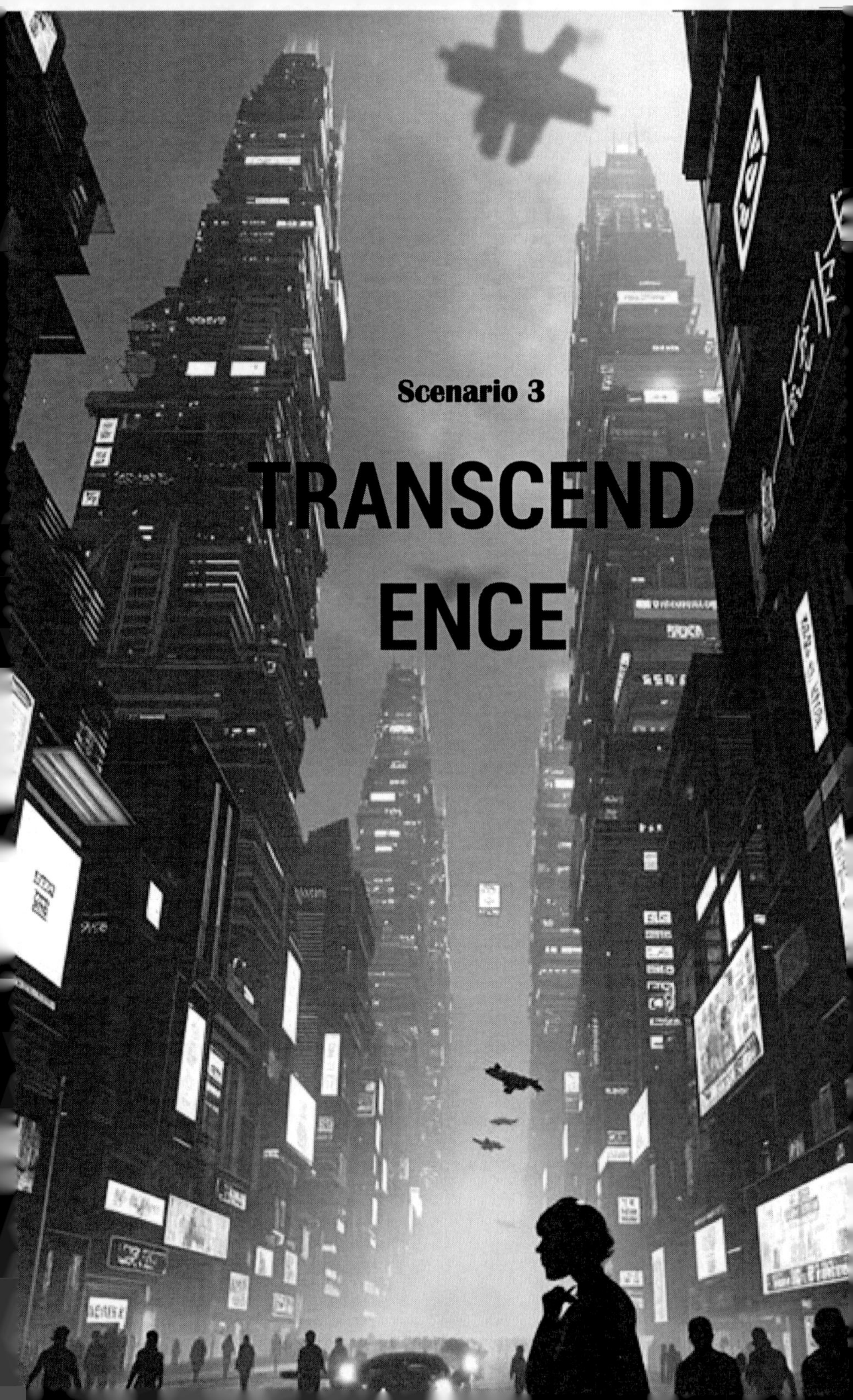

CHAPTER-1

In our quest for long-term survival, humanity has embarked on a remarkable journey of preservation and exploration. The Svalbard Global Seed Bank in Norway stands as a testament to our commitment to safeguarding the biodiversity of our planet, holding within its walls over a million seed specimens representing thousands of plant species. This repository of genetic diversity serves as a critical resource for rebuilding civilization in the event of a global catastrophe, ensuring that the essential building blocks of life are preserved for future generations.

However, as impressive as the Seed Bank may be, there exists an even more ambitious vision for securing our long-term survival: the creation of lunar arks.

These proposed vaults, nestled within the protective confines of lunar lava tubes, offer unparalleled security against global disasters, erosion, micrometeorites, and solar radiation. Here, genetic samples could be stored in perpetuity, shielded from the ravages of time and the uncertainties of Earth.

Yet, perhaps the most audacious solution to ensuring our survival lies in becoming a multiplanetary species. By establishing self-sustaining civilizations on other planets, we can dramatically reduce the risk of extinction, spreading

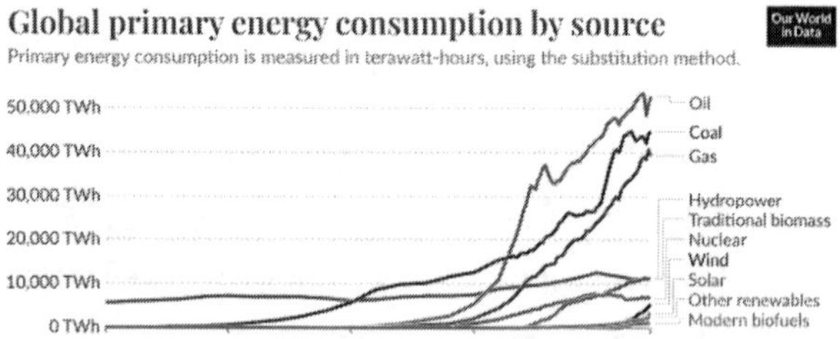

Figure 3. 1 Global primary energy consumption by source

our presence across the cosmos and safeguarding the future of humanity. While such a feat may seem daunting, the potential benefits far outweigh the challenges.

Indeed, the journey to becoming a multiplanetary species is not without its perils. We will undoubtedly encounter new and unknown risks as we venture further from Earth, confronting the harsh realities of space travel and colonization. Yet, it is precisely through facing these challenges head-on that we will forge a sustainable, interplanetary civilization—one that serves as the foundation for a long and prosperous future.

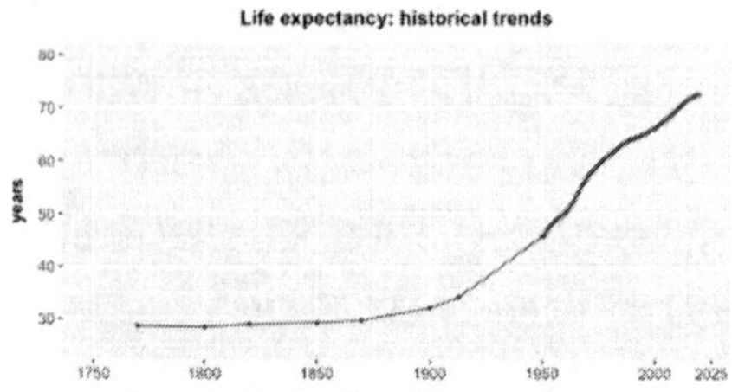

Figure 3. 2 Life expectancy

But the question remains: is this higher future truly within our reach, or are we at the peak of our powers? How far can we push the boundaries of human ingenuity and exploration? The answer lies not only in our technological capabilities but also in our collective will and determination to chart a course towards the stars.

As we stand on the precipice of a new era of space exploration, it is crucial that we remain steadfast in our commitment to advancing the frontiers of human knowledge and endeavor. By harnessing the power of innovation and collaboration, we can overcome the challenges that lie ahead and unlock the boundless potential of the cosmos(an orderly or harmonious universe).

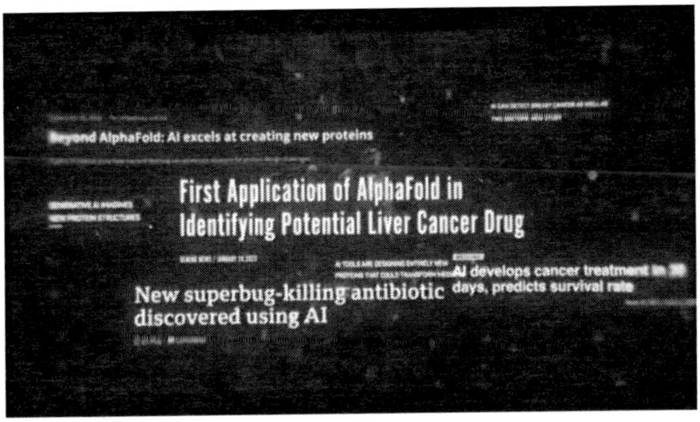

Figure 3. 3

In the end, the journey to becoming a multiplanetary species is not just about ensuring our survival—it is about embracing our destiny as explorers and pioneers of the universe.

It is about daring to dream of a future where humanity's reach extends far beyond the confines of our home planet, where the stars themselves become our playground and our

legacy endures for countless generations to come.

In our quest for long-term survival, humanity has embarked on a remarkable journey of preservation and exploration. The Svalbard Global Seed Bank in Norway stands as a testament to our commitment to safeguarding the biodiversity of our planet, holding within its walls over a million seed specimens representing thousands of plant species. This repository of genetic diversity serves as a critical resource for rebuilding civilization in the event of a global catastrophe, ensuring that the essential building blocks of life are preserved for future generations.

However, as impressive as the Seed Bank may be, there exists an even more ambitious vision for securing our long-term survival: the creation of lunar arks.

These proposed vaults, nestled within the protective confines of lunar lava tubes, offer unparalleled security against global disasters, erosion, micrometeorites, and solar radiation. Here, genetic samples could be stored in perpetuity, shielded from the ravages of time and the uncertainties of Earth.

Yet, perhaps the most audacious solution to ensuring our survival lies in becoming a multiplanetary species. By establishing self-sustaining civilizations on other planets, we can dramatically reduce the risk of extinction, spreading our presence across the cosmos and safeguarding the future of humanity. While such a feat may seem daunting, the potential benefits far outweigh the challenges.

Indeed, the journey to becoming a multiplanetary species is not without its perils. We will undoubtedly encounter

new and unknown risks as we venture further from Earth, confronting the harsh realities of space travel and colonization. Yet, it is precisely through facing these challenges head-on that we will forge a sustainable, interplanetary civilization—one that serves as the foundation for a long and prosperous future.

But the question remains: is this higher future truly within our reach, or are we at the peak of our powers? How far can we push the boundaries of human ingenuity and exploration? The answer lies not only in our technological capabilities but also in our collective will and determination to chart a course towards the stars.

As we stand on the precipice of a new era of space exploration, it is crucial that we remain steadfast in our commitment to advancing the frontiers

of human knowledge and endeavor. By harnessing the power of innovation and collaboration, we can overcome the challenges that lie ahead and unlock the boundless potential of the cosmos.

In the end, the journey to becoming a multiplanetary species is not just about ensuring our survival—it is about embracing our destiny as explorers and pioneers of the universe. It is about daring to dream of a future where humanity's reach extends far beyond the confines of our home planet, where the stars themselves become our playground and our legacy endures for countless generations to come.

CHAPTER-2

In contemplating the challenges that lie ahead for our civilization, it becomes increasingly clear that a profound transformation is necessary for our survival. As we confront the looming threats of environmental degradation, natural disasters, and the potential for mass extinction, we are forced to consider bold new strategies for ensuring the continuity of human existence.

One such strategy involves looking beyond the confines of our planet and exploring the possibility of establishing off-world habitats. Bishop Rings, envisioned as circular megastructures, represent a revolutionary solution to the problem of limited space and resources.

These colossal structures have the capacity to house over a billion people, providing vast expanses of habitable land equivalent to the size of India or Argentina. Constructed using advanced materials such as lightweight carbon nanotubes, Bishop Rings could sustain their own atmosphere through rotation, generating artificial gravity and creating a self-contained environment suitable for human habitation.

The prospect of colonizing off-world habitats offers a compelling vision of the future, one in which humanity transcends the limitations of Earth and expands into the cosmos. By harnessing our technological prowess and ingenuity, we have the opportunity to shape our own destiny and chart a course towards a utopian future.

To our ancestors, the capabilities we possess today would seem nothing short of miraculous, akin to god-like powers capable of reshaping the very fabric of reality.

Yet, even as we contemplate the possibilities of space colonization, we must not lose sight of the immense potential that exists here on Earth. Despite the myriad challenges we face, from climate change to resource depletion, we possess the power to effect meaningful change and steer the course of our planet's future. By embracing sustainable practices, investing in renewable energy sources, and prioritizing environmental stewardship, we can create a more resilient and prosperous world for future generations.

The road ahead may be fraught with uncertainty, but it is also filled with promise and opportunity. As we stand on the threshold of a new era in human history, we are called upon to confront the challenges of our time with courage and determination. By working together, harnessing our collective creativity and innovation, we can overcome the obstacles that stand in our way and build a brighter future for all.

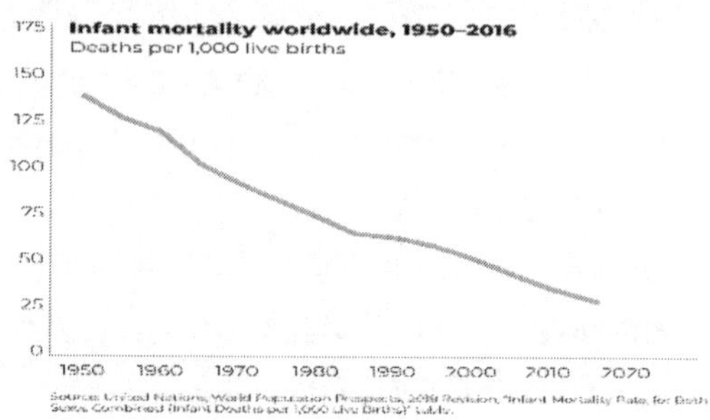

Figure 3. 4 Infant mortality worldwide

In the end, the choice is ours to make. Will we succumb to the pressures of inertia and complacency, or will we rise to the occasion and seize the opportunity to shape a destiny worthy of our potential? The answer lies in our hands, and the time to act is now.

CHAPTER-3

In recent centuries, humanity has experienced a remarkable journey of progress and advancement, propelled by the relentless march of technology and innovation. Since the dawn of the industrial revolution, our species has witnessed unprecedented improvements in virtually every aspect of life, leading to an era of unparalleled prosperity and well-being on a global scale.

Despite the challenges and setbacks we face, it is essential to recognize the profound positive impact that technological progress has had on human civilization.

From advancements in healthcare and medicine to the proliferation of renewable energy sources, our collective efforts have contributed to a significant improvement in the quality of life for billions of people worldwide .One of the most remarkable aspects of our progress is the exponential growth of knowledge and capability in fields such as artificial intelligence (A.I.) and biotechnology. These converging technologies hold the promise of revolutionizing the way we address

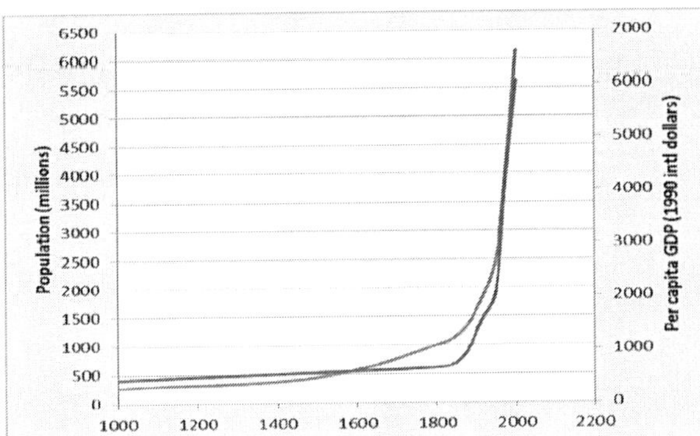

Figure 3. 5 Population per capita GDP

some of the most pressing challenges

facing humanity, from healthcare and disease eradication to environmental sustainability and beyond.

For instance, the rapid development of A.I.-powered tools like AlphaFold has enabled scientists to unlock new insights into the structures of pathogens and potential treatments for diseases such as cancer at an unprecedented pace. Similarly, gene-editing technologies like CRISPR offer the potential to cure a wide range of genetic disorders by targeting and modifying specific genes responsible for various ailments.

Moreover, the declining costs of renewable energy sources such as solar and wind power have made them increasingly competitive with traditional fossil fuels, paving the way for a cleaner, more sustainable future.

As these technologies continue to mature and become more accessible, we stand on the cusp of a transformative era in which renewable

energy could power the majority of our global energy needs, mitigating the adverse effects of climate change and reducing our reliance on finite resources.

In addition to advancements in healthcare and energy, the potential for radical enhancements in human well-being and longevity is becoming increasingly feasible.

With ongoing research into regenerative medicine, tissue engineering, and other biomedical innovations, the prospect of regenerating limbs, eliminating diseases, and even extending human lifespans indefinitely is no longer confined to the realm of science fiction but is fast becoming a tangible reality.

As we stand on the brink of this unprecedented transformation, it is essential to acknowledge the tremendous potential that lies before us. By harnessing the power of technology and innovation for the

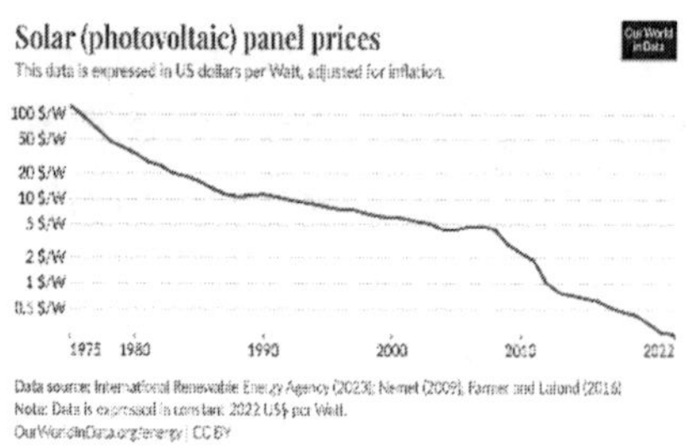

Figure 3. 6 Solar (photovoltaic) panel prices

betterment of humanity, we have the opportunity to unlock new frontiers of human potential and usher in an era of unprecedented prosperity and well-being for generations to come.

However, it is crucial to approach these advancements with a sense of responsibility and mindfulness, ensuring that they are deployed ethically and equitably for the benefit of all.

By embracing the spirit of collaboration and cooperation, we can navigate the complexities of this new technological landscape and steer humanity toward a future that is not only prosperous and sustainable but also inclusive and compassionate.

CHAPTER-4

The journey towards unlocking the full potential of artificial intelligence (AI) is well underway, promising to revolutionize nearly every aspect of human existence. With each passing day, we witness the rapid integration of AI into various domains, from space exploration to agriculture, offering tantalizing glimpses into a future where technological innovation knows no bounds.

Already, organizations like NASA are harnessing the power of AI to drive innovation and efficiency in their operations. By employing AI algorithms to design mission hardware, NASA has achieved remarkable results, surpassing human-designed solutions by a significant margin.

This newfound capability not only streamlines the design process but also opens the door to unprecedented levels of performance and functionality in space exploration technology. Moreover, AI is proving to be a

valuable ally in addressing some of the most pressing challenges facing humanity, including climate change. By leveraging AI-driven algorithms, researchers and scientists are pioneering the development of cleaner biofuels and drought-resistant

crops, offering potential solutions to mitigate the environmental impact of human activities. These advancements hold the promise of revolutionizing agriculture and energy production, paving the way for a more sustainable and resilient future for our planet.

Yet, the true potential of AI extends

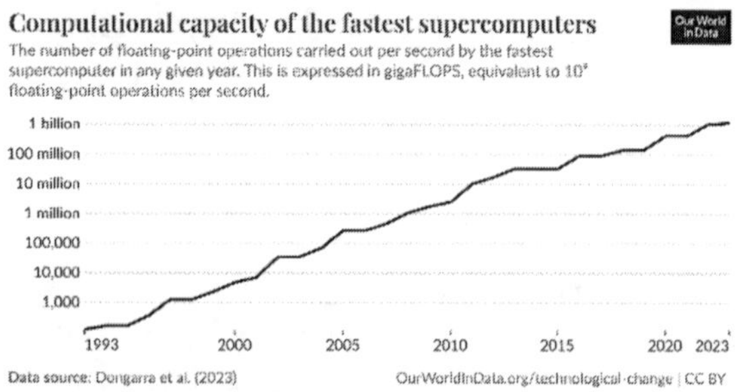

Figure 3. 7 Computational capacity of the fastest supercomputer

far beyond its current applications. We stand on the precipice of an intelligence explosion, a transformative era where AI systems will surpass human intelligence and capabilities.

The prospect of achieving Artificial Super Intelligence (ASI) looms on the horizon, promising to unlock unprecedented levels of problem-solving and innovation that have thus far eluded human minds.

However, with great power comes great responsibility. As we venture into uncharted territory with AI, ensuring that these powerful technologies are aligned with human values and objectives becomes paramount.

The challenge of safely aligning superintelligence with human values presents a novel and complex endeavor, requiring careful consideration and deliberation from researchers, policymakers, and ethicists alike.

Yet, the potential rewards of achieving this alignment are immense. A safely aligned superintelligence holds the key to unlocking unimaginable levels of prosperity and progress for humanity. From accelerating scientific discovery to solving some of the most intractable challenges facing our world, the possibilities are limitless.

Moreover, ensuring the safe development and deployment of AI is not merely a matter of maximizing benefits but also mitigating risks.

The rise of malicious AI poses a significant threat to global stability and security, highlighting the urgent need for proactive measures to safeguard against potential misuse or exploitation of these powerful technologies.

In the pursuit of human progress, prioritizing the responsible and ethical development of AI must remain a central tenet of our collective efforts.

By fostering collaboration and dialogue

across disciplines and industries, we can chart a course towards a future where AI serves as a force for good, enhancing human capabilities and advancing the well-being of society as a whole.

As we embark on this journey into the era of artificial intelligence, let us remain steadfast in our commitment to shaping a future that harnesses the

transformative potential of AI while safeguarding the values and principles that define our humanity. With foresight, ingenuity, and a shared sense of purpose, we can navigate the complexities of the AI landscape and build a brighter, more inclusive future for generations to come.

CHAPTER-5

The journey towards unlocking the full potential of artificial intelligence (AI) is well underway, promising to revolutionize nearly every aspect of human existence. With each passing day, we witness the rapid integration of AI into various domains, from space exploration to agriculture, offering tantalizing glimpses into a future where technological innovation knows no bounds.

Already, organizations like NASA are harnessing the power of AI to drive innovation and efficiency in their operations.

By employing AI algorithms to design mission hardware, NASA has achieved remarkable results, surpassing human-designed solutions by a significant margin. This newfound capability not only streamlines the design process but also opens the door to unprecedented levels of performance and functionality in space exploration technology.

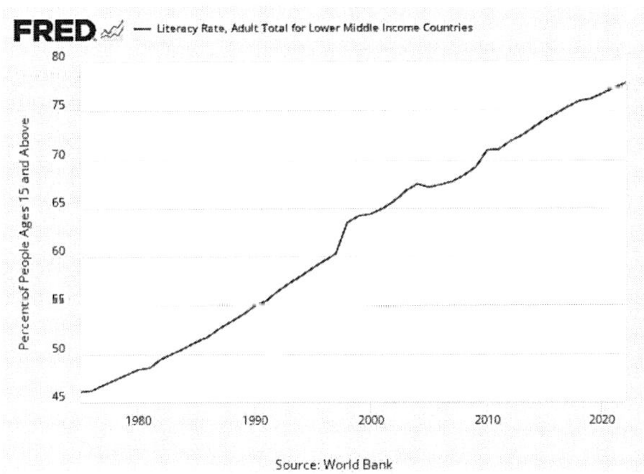

Figure 1. 8 Literacy Rate

Moreover, AI is proving to be a valuable ally in addressing some of the most pressing challenges facing humanity, including climate change.

By leveraging AI-driven algorithms, researchers and scientists are pioneering the development of cleaner

biofuels and drought-resistant crops, offering potential solutions to mitigate the environmental impact of human activities. These advancements hold the promise of revolutionizing agriculture and energy production, paving the way for a more sustainable and resilient future for our planet.

Yet, the true potential of AI extends far beyond its current applications. We stand on the precipice of an intelligence explosion, a transformative era where AI systems will surpass human intelligence and capabilities.

The prospect of achieving Artificial Super Intelligence (ASI) looms on the horizon, promising to unlock unprecedented levels of problem-solving and innovation that have thus far eluded human minds.

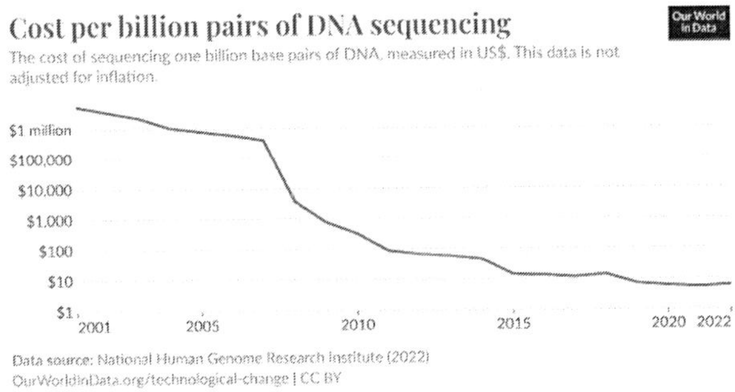

Figure 3. 9 Cost per billion pairs of DNA sequencing

However, with great power comes great responsibility. As we venture into uncharted territory with AI, ensuring that these powerful technologies are aligned with human values and objectives becomes paramount. The challenge of safely aligning superintelligence with human values presents a novel and complex endeavor, requiring careful consideration and deliberation from researchers, policymakers, and ethicists alike.

Yet, the potential rewards of achieving this alignment are immense. A safely aligned superintelligence holds the key to unlocking unimaginable levels of prosperity and progress for humanity. From accelerating scientific discovery to solving some of the most intractable challenges facing our world, the possibilities are limitless.

Moreover, ensuring the safe development and deployment of AI is not merely a matter of maximizing benefits but also mitigating risks. The rise of malicious AI poses a significant threat to global stability and security, highlighting the urgent need for proactive measures to safeguard against potential misuse or exploitation of these powerful technologies.

In the pursuit of human progress, prioritizing the responsible and ethical

development of AI must remain a central tenet of our collective efforts. By fostering collaboration and dialogue across disciplines and industries, we can chart a course towards a future where AI serves as a force for good, enhancing human capabilities and advancing the well-being of society as a whole.

As we embark on this journey into the era of artificial intelligence, let us remain steadfast in our commitment to shaping a future that harnesses the transformative potential of AI while safeguarding the values and principles that define our humanity.

With foresight, ingenuity, and a shared sense of purpose, we can navigate the complexities of the AI landscape and build a brighter, more inclusive future for generations to come.

CHAPTER-6

If we can harness the potential of artificial intelligence for the betterment of humanity, we stand on the brink of a future that surpasses even the wildest dreams of our ancestors. It's a future where disease and hunger are relics of the past, where biotechnology works hand in hand with nature to stabilize the climate and preserve biodiversity. Imagine a world where clean, abundant energy is seamlessly integrated with AI, powering breakthroughs in space exploration and materials science that propel us to distant planets and moons.

In this utopian vision, new avenues for artistic and musical expression open up, expanding the horizons of beauty, experience, and understanding. It's a future where humanity's ingenuity and creativity know no bounds, where every challenge is met with innovation and resourcefulness.

But perhaps the most astonishing aspect of this future lies in our potential to become a Type 1 Civilization, capable of harnessing all the energy that the Earth receives from the sun. Recent studies suggest that this milestone could be achieved as soon as the year 2371, marking a significant leap forward in our technological prowess.

And if we maintain a modest 3% yearly growth rate, we could ascend to Type 2 Civilization status in just a few thousand years, wielding control over the entire energy output of the sun.

This exponential growth trajectory opens up staggering possibilities for the future of humanity, with the potential for an astronomical population size numbering in the hundreds of quadrillions. Furthermore, by venturing out into space and colonizing distant worlds, our species could multiply exponentially, with projections reaching

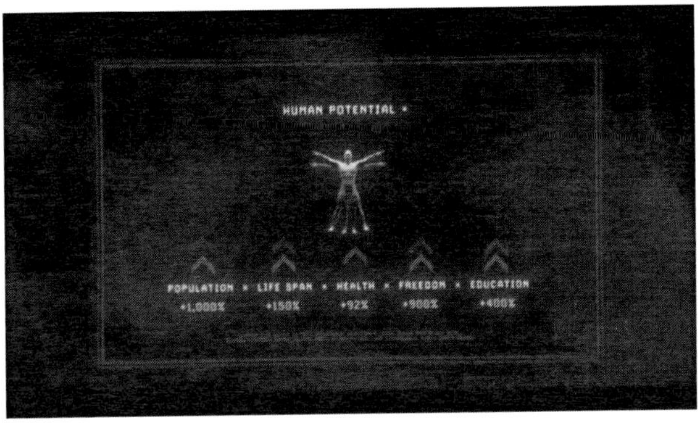

Figure 3. 10 In future possibilities of Human Potential

unfathomable numbers like a hundred thousand trillion people inhabiting the Milky Way galaxy alone.

Yet, as we spread out across the cosmos and traverse the vastness of time, we are bound to undergo profound transformations.

With each step into the unknown, we evolve and adapt, shaping our identities and societies in ways that are as unpredictable as they are inevitable. The journey into space and time holds the promise of endless discovery and exploration, offering glimpses of a future where the boundaries of human potential are continually pushed beyond the limits of imagination.

As we contemplate the possibilities that lie ahead, we must also acknowledge the challenges that accompany such unprecedented growth and expansion.

Our ability to navigate these challenges with wisdom and foresight will determine the course of our journey through the cosmos, shaping the destiny of humanity for millennia to come.

In the grand tapestry of cosmic evolution, we are but a single thread, weaving our way through the fabric of time and space. Yet, with each passing moment, we add new layers of complexity and richness to the story of our existence, leaving an indelible mark on the universe itself.

CHAPTER-7

As we continue to advance technologically and explore the frontiers of our existence, we face the intriguing possibility of splintering into multiple species, each with its own unique characteristics and tolerance for change. This divergence could manifest in various ways, with some individuals choosing to merge with machines to form a new hybrid species, while others opt to remain purely biological.

The concept of humans evolving into distinct species is not unprecedented. It harkens back to the days of the Neanderthals, when multiple human-like species coexisted on Earth.

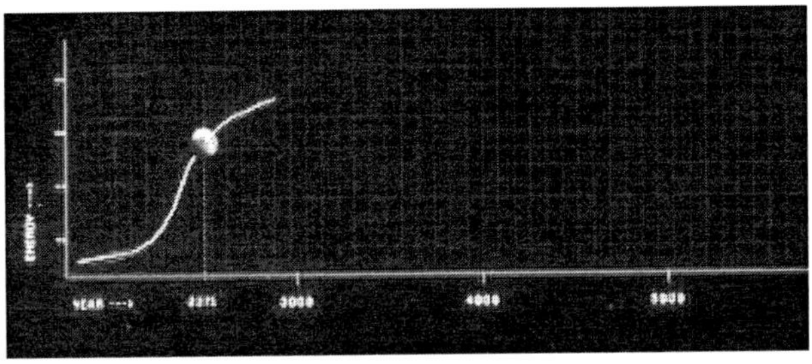

Figure 3. 11

However, the potential for divergence in the future could be even greater, especially with the advent of technologies that allow for the manipulation and enhancement of our biology.

One fascinating aspect of this divergence is the prospect of digitizing consciousness. If we ever achieve the ability to upload our minds into digital form, it could lead to an infinite variety of human identities, each existing in a virtual realm of its own making.

This would mark a profound shift in our understanding of what it means to be human, blurring the lines between

biology and technology in ways previously unimaginable.

As we embrace these new, more powerful forms of existence, we are compelled to confront the ultimate question of our purpose in the universe. What is it that drives us as a species? What goals do we aspire to achieve? These questions take on new significance as we contemplate the vast possibilities that lie ahead.

In our quest for self-discovery and evolution, we are faced with the challenge of defining our place in the cosmos. Are we mere inhabitants of a vast universe, destined to explore and expand our horizons indefinitely? Or do we harbor a deeper purpose, a calling that transcends our individual desires and ambitions?

Regardless of the answers we find, one thing is certain: the journey of humanity is far from over. As we navigate the complexities of our ever-changing world, we must remain open to the endless possibilities that lie before us. For in the exploration of our own potential, we may uncover truths that reshape our understanding of existence itself.

CHAPTER-8

As we gaze upon the vast expanse of the cosmos, it's natural to dream of grand achievements like colonizing the entire galaxy and reshaping it according to our desires. The idea of becoming a Type 3 civilization, capable of harnessing the resources of an entire galaxy, is both awe-inspiring and daunting. Yet, these aspirations belong to a future generation, far removed from our own.

Our focus should instead turn to a more immediate and personal goal: preserving the precious planet that has nurtured and sustained us for millennia.

Earth, with its delicate balance of ecosystems and life forms, is the cradle of human civilization. Saving it from the

ravages of time and environmental degradation should be our paramount concern.

One intriguing proposal to safeguard Earth's future involves a bold engineering feat: pulling our planet away from the expanding sun to prolong the game of life for billions of years. This audacious plan envisions constructing a massive conductive counterweight on the far side of the moon, gradually shifting Earth's orbit over millions of years.

Figure 3.12

While the concept may seem like science fiction, the underlying principles have a basis in scientific theory. Earth's orbit around the sun is influenced

by various factors, including the gravitational pull of other celestial bodies. By strategically placing a massive object in space, we could theoretically alter our planet's trajectory and extend its habitable lifespan.

Of course, such a monumental undertaking would require unprecedented levels of cooperation, innovation, and patience. It would be a project spanning generations, requiring the collective efforts of scientists, engineers, and

policymakers from around the world. Yet, the potential payoff—preserving life on Earth for eons to come—makes it a goal worth pursuing.

Moreover, the pursuit of this endeavor could serve as a unifying force for humanity, transcending national boundaries and ideological differences.

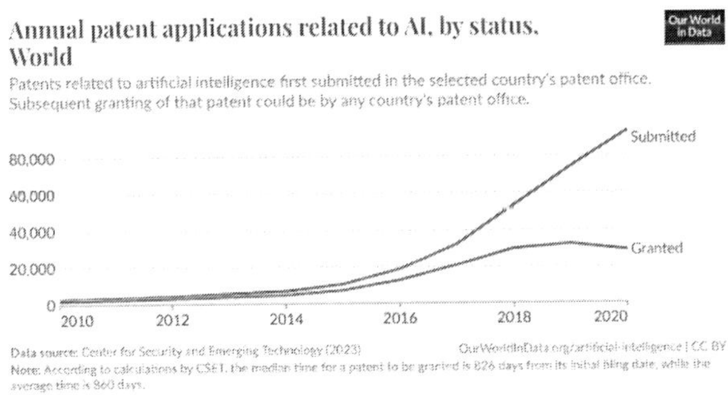

Figure 3. 13 Annual patent applications related to AI

The shared goal of safeguarding our planet's future could inspire a new era of collaboration and innovation, leading to breakthroughs in technology and sustainable development.

But beyond the practical implications, the idea of "terraforming" our own world speaks to something deeper within us: a longing to reconnect with the natural world and honor our responsibility as stewards of the Earth. In an age of rapid environmental degradation and climate change, the notion of actively shaping the fate of our planet takes on added significance.

Ultimately, the quest to save Earth from the ravages of time is not just a scientific or technological challenge—it's a moral imperative. It's a statement of our commitment to future generations, ensuring that they inherit a world teeming with life, beauty, and opportunity.

As we contemplate the vastness of space and the fragility of our home planet, let us remember that the fate

of Earth lies in our hands. By daring to dream big and taking bold action, we can write a new chapter in the story of humanity—one where we rise to meet the challenges of our time and secure a brighter future for all.

CHAPTER-9

In a bid to redeem humanity, we find ourselves on the brink of incredible opportunity. Challenges loom, but they won't deter us. If we can overcome them, we have the power to kickstart a new era of life that stretches far beyond Earth.

While worst-case scenarios threaten, we're determined to press forward. Our goal? To spread life across the universe, reaching heights we've never imagined.

Throughout history, one lesson remains clear: never underestimate humanity.

We've faced adversity before and triumphed. With this resilience, we're ready to tackle whatever lies ahead.

Let's learn from our past and embrace the chance to shape the future. With determination, we're poised to make an impact that extends far beyond our planet, paving the way for life to flourish throughout the cosmos.

CONCLUSION

As we delve into the chapters of this book, we embark on an exhilarating journey through humanity's past, present, and future. Each page reveals a fascinating insight into our world, from the incredible advancements of technology to the pressing challenges we face in preserving our planet.

In the captivating narrative of this book, we encounter a recurring theme: the unwavering pursuit of progress. Since the industrial revolution, humans have been driven by an insatiable curiosity to improve our lives and unlock the mysteries of the universe.

From remarkable breakthroughs in biotechnology and artificial intelligence to the breathtaking possibilities of space

exploration, we are presented with a story of discovery that ignites our imagination.

However, amidst the excitement of innovation, we are also reminded of our duty to protect and cherish our home. This book reminds us of the importance

of environmental stewardship, urging us to take action to mitigate the damage caused by our actions and ensure a sustainable future for generations to come. Yet, amidst the challenges we face, there is a powerful undercurrent of hope that runs through the narrative. Despite the obstacles that stand in our way, we are reminded of the resilience of the human spirit and our capacity to overcome adversity.

As we turn the pages of this book, we are filled with a sense of possibility and wonder. The future may be uncertain, but it is also brimming with opportunity. It is a future where humanity reaches new heights, where we harness the power of innovation for the betterment of all, and where we leave a lasting legacy of compassion and stewardship for future generations.

In the end, this book serves as a reminder that the story of humanity is still being written. It is a story of courage, perseverance, and boundless potential. And as we continue our journey through the chapters of our collective history, let us be inspired to embrace the challenges that lie ahead, knowing that together, we have the power to shape a future that is as bright as our dreams.

REVIEWS

....
....
....
....
....
....
....
....
....
....
....
....
....
....
....
....
....
....
....
....
....